TALKING IT THROUGH

I can't hear like you

Althea

Illustrated by Bridget Dowty

000000522990

I can't hear very well - I am deaf.
I wear a hearing aid behind each ear to help me
hear better.

My hearing aids make all noises louder. They help me to hear what people are saying, but their voices get a bit mixed up and I can hear lots of other noises too.

I have to watch very carefully when people are speaking. It helps if they are looking at me when they speak. I can lipread some of the words, but it can be confusing, as some of the sounds are difficult to see and many words look the same.

I guess at some of the words and I can usually tell by people's faces when they are serious or if they are making a joke.

Can you lipread? Try by turning the sound down on the television or cover up your ears and see if you can see what people are saying. It's hard to do, isn't it?

hello

My friend David is profoundly deaf which means that he can hear very little at all, even with his hearing aids. He uses sign language at home and at school. But it's hard when he's with people who can't sign. He finds it very difficult to lipread, and he sounds funny when he talks because he can't hear how he is speaking.

I am learning sign language so I can talk to him and my other friends who are deaf. I think more people should learn to talk with their hands. It's fun and it stops people who can't hear from being left out.

At school I have some of my lessons in a class with other children who wear hearing aids.

Some children have a cochlear implant instead of hearing aids. The microphone picks up the sounds. The speech processor is a small computer. It sorts and sends the sounds to the transmitter.

microphone

speech processor

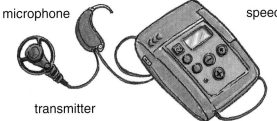

transmitter

The transmitter is attached to the head by a magnet. It sends the sounds to a tiny magnetic receiver under the skin.

microphone

These are like my hearing aids, but they have red moulds.

This tiny radio aid can be attached to a hearing aid. I hope I can have one like that one day.

This is like the transmitter I give to the teacher when I go to other classes.

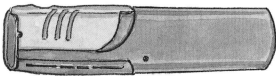

The teacher can wear this transmitter, or put it on the table in front of her.

When I go to other classes with children who can hear, I attach a radio aid to my hearing aids. I give the teacher a transmitter with a microphone to wear, and then I sit at the front, so I can lipread too.

If the teacher moves about I sometimes miss what she is saying and have to ask her to say it again.

It is difficult when lots of people talk, or when someone asks a question. I can't know who will say something next, so I don't always turn quickly enough to see what they say. It helps when the teacher repeats the question.

When we go swimming, I have to take off my hearing aids to stop them getting wet. It means I can't hear the teacher, so I watch everyone else and copy what they are doing.

When I first came to this school, some of the children used to tease and bully me. They said I was stupid because I didn't always understand them, and because I don't speak very clearly. It made me want to hit them.

Now I have my own friends and I like playing with them. Sometimes the shouting and loud noises in the playground hurts my ears, so I turn down my hearing aids.

When I am very tired of trying to listen I switch off my aids or take them out. Then I can sit and read a book, or play a game on my own.

I like it when we work on the computers.
I can do the work just as well as anybody,
because it tells me what to do on the
screen, and I don't have to listen to
anybody. Some computers make my
hearing aids hum, which is a nuisance.

I think I would like to work with computers when I grow up.

computer

internet

e-mail

disk

I take off my hearing aids at night. I used to get frightened in the dark when everything went so quiet. But I like it now. If my baby brother cries at night mum or dad comes in to look after him, and I don't hear anything.

night

In the morning, mum shakes my arm to wake me up. I might ask for a flashing alarm clock for my birthday. On the night before I go to the hearing clinic, mum puts a few drops of olive oil in my ears. It softens the wax, so when I have a shower in the morning, it washes out.

morning

I go to the hearing clinic about twice a year, so they can check my hearing. I take off my hearing aids and put on some earphones. The doctor asks me to press the button when I hear a sound. Some of the sounds are very tiny, and I have to listen hard to hear them.

Next, to make sure my hearing aids are still right for me, I put them on again, and press the button when I hear noises coming through the loudspeakers.

When I was younger I had to put a toy man in a boat, or bricks in a basket, when I heard a sound.

My hearing aids still work well, but I need new ear moulds, because my ears are growing and changing shape. The doctor puts a little sponge in my ear with a length of cotton attached to it. The sponge stops the mould from going in too far, and the cotton makes it easy to pull it out when the mould has set.

The doctor makes a blue putty-like mixture,
which she squirts into my ear. She gives me the
remains of the stuff to play with while it goes hard.

She'll send the moulds off to have proper moulds made.
I could have coloured moulds, or even sparkly ones, but
I think I'll stick to white. The doctor will post them to
me in a week or so.

We took my baby brother to the hearing clinic and they did some tests to see if he could hear properly. Each time a sound was made he turned to see where the noise was coming from and a puppet jumped up and down in a box, and made him laugh.

They said he could hear very well. We were all pleased.

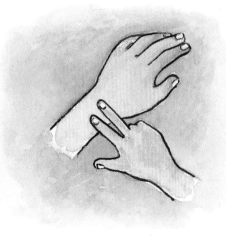

doctor

old

My gran can't hear very well. She has a hearing aid too. She says lots of people can't hear very well when they get older.

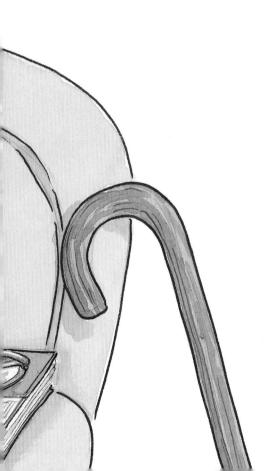

Gran says people don't always understand, and they can be a bit impatient and unkind. Sometimes they laugh at you, when you get what they say wrong. She's right.

Friends can help me a lot when we work or play together. They can tell me what is happening when I get confused by all the different noises, or I miss what someone is saying because I am not looking at the person who is speaking.

Some of them think I talk in a funny way, but they soon get used to it.

goodbye

Some people think you must be stupid if you wear a hearing aid. People don't think you are stupid if you wear headphones to listen to your cassette or CD player.

Silly, isn't it?

The author and illustrator would like to thank the following
people who helped in the production of this book:
The audiology department at Addenbrooke's Hospital,
Cambridge. The National Deaf Children's Society.
The Librarian and staff at the RNID
(The Royal National Institute for Deaf People),
and the Hearing Support Unit at
Mayfield Primary School, Cambridge.

Published by
Happy Cat Books
An imprint of Catnip Publishing Ltd
14 Greville Street
London EC1N 8SB

This edition published 2001
3 5 7 9 10 8 6 4 2

Text copyright © Althea Braithwaite, 1985, 2001
Illustrations copyright © Bridget Dowty, 2001
The moral rights of the author and illustrator have been asserted
All rights reserved

A CIP catalogue record for this book is available from the British Library

ISBN: 978-1-903285-06-0

Printed in China

www.catnippublishing.co.uk